DOCUMENTED BRIEFING

RAND

Unequal Wealth and Incentives to Save

James P. Smith

This research was supported by RAND using its own funds.

ISBN: 0-8330-2289-X

The RAND documented briefing series is a mechanism for timely, easy-to-read reporting of research that has been briefed to the client and possibly to other audiences. Although documented briefings have been formally reviewed, they are not expected to be comprehensive or definitive. In many cases, they represent interim work.

RAND is a nonprofit institution that helps improve public policy through research and analysis. RAND's publications do not necessarily reflect the opinions or policies of its research sponsors.

Published 1995 by RAND
1700 Main Street, P.O. Box 2138, Santa Monica, CA 90407-2138
RAND URL: http://www.rand.org/
To order RAND documents or to obtain additional information, contact Distribution
Services: Telephone: (310) 451-7002; Fax: (310) 451-6915; Internet: order@rand.org/

DOCUMENTED BRIEFING

RAND

Unequal Wealth and Incentives to Save

James P. Smith

PREFACE

The most critical domestic problems this country faces are large and rising inequities in economic resources, a low savings rate and little economic growth, and Social Security and Medicare commitments that are simply impossible to honor. This briefing provides new evidence about the magnitude of these problems and their likely underlying causes and outlines some possible solutions. This briefing was initially presented to the RAND Board of Trustees at their April 1995 meeting.

James P. Smith is a senior economist at RAND and holds the RAND Chair in Demographic and Labor Market Studies. Funds from this Chair were used to prepare this briefing and to convert it into this document. The research upon which this briefing is based was supported by grants from the National Institute on Aging and the National Institute of Child Health and Human Development. The research papers that underlie this briefing are listed in the bibliography. Helpful comments on an earlier draft were made by RAND staff Lynn Karoly and Linda Martin.

Policy Issues

- **Are households saving enough for their retirement years?**

- **Does our current Social Security system reduce private savings?**

- **Do our existing safety net programs encourage the poor not to save?**

- **How important are inheritances in solidifying inequalities across generations?**

This briefing examines the extent of wealth inequality in the United States and documents wealth disparities across racial and ethnic groups. In doing so, it touches on a number of critical policy issues of the day. These issues are guaranteed to dominate the domestic public policy discussion for the next few decades. This guarantee is easy to make in the face of the awesome demographic aging of our population and our current political inability to make a down payment on some solutions. These issues revolve around the following: Do households save enough for their retirement years, does our current Social Security system reduce private savings and thereby contribute to our low national savings rate, do our existing safety net programs encourage the poor not to save, and finally how important are inheritances in solidifying inequalities across generations?

The briefing is organized into three parts. The first describes the data that were used, the groups that were studied, and how wealth was defined. The second part isolates the most salient characteristics of wealth distributions in America. How much wealth inequality is there? And who has this wealth and who doesn't? The final and most important part of the briefing focuses on the critical substantive issue—why do so many American households, particularly the less well-to-do ones, save so little for their retirement or for other emergencies?

1

```
┌─────────────────────────────────────────────────────────┐
│                                                           │
│             Data Resources for the Study                 │
│                                                           │
│                                                           │
│   • Health and Retirement Survey  (1993)                  │
│                                                           │
│        – 7,600 households and 12,654 individuals ages 51-61│
│                                                           │
│        – Income, wealth, labor force participation, and   │
│          physical and mental health status and disabilities│
│                                                           │
│        – Oversamples of blacks and Hispanics              │
│                                                           │
│   • Asset and Health Dynamics of Oldest-Old (1994)        │
│                                                           │
│        – 6,052 households and 8,223 individuals aged 70+   │
│                                                           │
│        – Income; wealth; physical, emotional, cognitive   │
│          capacity; intergenerational transfers            │
│                                                           │
│        – Oversamples of blacks and Hispanics              │
│                                                           │
└─────────────────────────────────────────────────────────┘
```

My research relies on two important new national surveys recently funded by the National Institute on Aging (NIA) and fielded by the Institute for Survey Research at the University of Michigan. The first—the Health and Retirement Survey (HRS)—contains more than 7,600 households with at least one person in their fifties.[1] Given that age span, not surprisingly, its substantive focus is on transitions into retirement and the adequacy of past household savings to provide a comfortable living during the retirement years. The second survey—Asset and Health Dynamics of Oldest-Old (AHEAD)—contains over 6,000 households with one member at least 70 years old.[2] The objective of this survey is to monitor the adequacy of economic resources during the time when many people of this age are at risk of serious physical and cognitive impairment. Both surveys contain oversamples of black and Hispanic households, and follow-ups are planned at two-year intervals.

Given the age groups of these two surveys, this briefing will present data only on two important age cohorts—a cohort of those nearing retirement (in their fifties) and another postretirement-age cohort (at least age 70).

---

[1]For a detailed description of the HRS design, see Juster and Suzman (1995).

[2]For a detailed description of the AHEAD design, see Hurd et al. (1994).

Comprehensive Concepts of Wealth Are Used

- **Household wealth**
  - **Net housing value**
    (home value – all mortgages)
    plus
  - **Real assets**
    (other real estate, cars, business equity)
    plus
  - **Financial assets**
    (IRA/Keogh, stocks, trusts, mutual funds, savings accounts, certificates of deposit, treasury bills, other liquid assets
    minus **other debts)**
- **Total wealth**
  - **Household wealth**
    plus
  - **Discounted value of all future social security benefits**
    plus
  - **Discounted value of all future private pension benefits**

Although this age restriction is dictated in part by data limitations, these are critical age groups when investigating the adequacy of savings for retirement, an essential motivation for private household savings. To avoid repeating the main conclusions each time for each of the two age cohorts, data will often be presented for only one age group. When this is done, the implication will always be that the same pattern prevails for the other age group.

Both surveys have in common comprehensive and high-quality measures of household wealth. In this briefing, two concepts of wealth will be used. The first—household wealth—includes any equity held in all homes, the value of business and other real assets, and a very detailed list of financial assets. These financial assets span checking and savings accounts, stocks and bonds, along with the other financial instruments listed in this chart. Household wealth is the traditional definition of wealth; the difference here is that we have household surveys devoted to high-quality measurement of these concepts. [3]

Despite its widespread use, household wealth often ignores large components of wealth that are critical to many households. For example, a household's future expected Social Security benefits can be thought of as

3

a lifetime annuity that can be discounted to give a present value of Social Security wealth. In a similar vein, private pensions, either directly in defined contribution plans or indirectly for defined benefit plans, are an important source of wealth for many households. Total wealth will be defined as the sum of household wealth, Social Security wealth, and private pension wealth.[4]

In the first part of the briefing, I will rely only on the conventional definition of wealth, and all data presented will refer to household wealth. Later I will demonstrate how my conclusions will be altered if the broader concept of total wealth is used.

---

[3]For an overall picture of wealth disparities and trends for all age groups, see Wolff (1994).

[4]For the details involved in the construction of these wealth measures, see Smith (1995a, 1995c). For an evaluation of the quality of the wealth data, see Juster and Smith (1995).

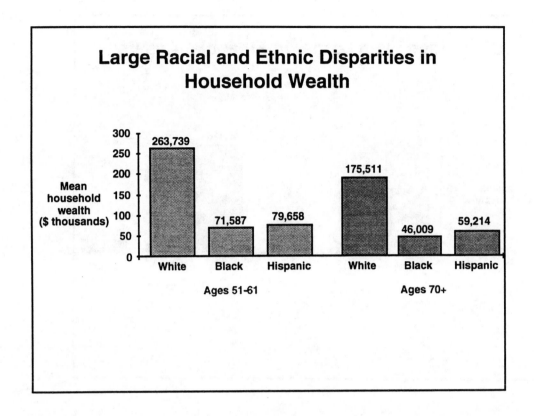

Large Racial and Ethnic Disparities in Household Wealth

Mean household wealth ($ thousands)

Ages 51-61: White 263,739; Black 71,587; Hispanic 79,658

Ages 70+: White 175,511; Black 46,009; Hispanic 59,214

We know a good deal about income differences, but because of the current lack of good data we know amazingly little about how much personal wealth people have access to and how and why that wealth is distributed.

Mean household wealth is a little more than a quarter of a million dollars for households of middle-aged whites, while white households headed by people over 70 years old have about $175,000. Their lower assets reflect both some asset depletion in old age, but mostly the fact that those in the younger age group were born 25 years later and hence are members of much wealthier cohorts who experienced greater economic prosperity.

Race and ethnic disparities are enormous, far out distancing any other income differences that exist among these groups. For example, for every dollar of wealth of a white household of those in middle age, black households have 27 cents and Hispanic households have 30 cents on the dollar.[5] These wealth gaps compare with racial income ratios of about 60 percent in these age groups. One of the central puzzles we must resolve is why racial and ethnic disparities in *wealth* are so much larger than those that exist in *incomes*.

---

[5]The racial and ethnic wealth gaps are quite similar to these in the older age group.

5

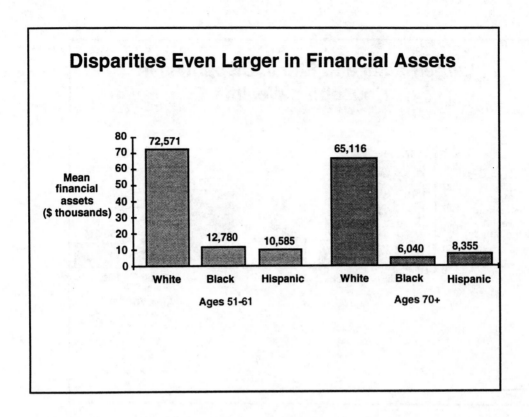

Disparities Even Larger in Financial Assets

Mean financial assets ($ thousands)

Ages 51-61: White 72,571; Black 12,780; Hispanic 10,585

Ages 70+: White 65,116; Black 6,040; Hispanic 8,355

These racial and ethnic disparities are even larger when we concentrate on financial assets only. Remember financial assets are defined quite broadly, excluding only housing and other real assets. These remaining more-liquid assets may be a better index of how many resources a household has on hand to meet emergencies. If they are a better index, the problems many minority households face are apparent. Among those over 70, for example, black households have less than one-tenth the financial assets of white households. Hispanic households fare little better, with only one-eighth the financial assets of whites. Although racial and ethnic disparities in financial wealth are somewhat smaller among households of those in their fifties, the disparities remain enormous.

Household Wealth Is Unequally Distributed

Percentiles of household wealth	Household wealth in $ (ages 70+)		
	White	Black	Hispanic
10	765	0	0
20	13,000	0	0
30	38,000	700	0
50	90,000	17,000	14,400
70	170,050	45,000	47,000
90	413,000	114,600	138,000
95	655,000	182,000	226,000
Mean	*175,511*	*46,009*	*59,214*

As large as these disparities may seem, they are actually seriously understated by the use of means. This chart displays household wealth levels at selected deciles of the full wealth distribution.[6] To ease comparisons, mean wealth is repeated in the last row at the bottom. In contrast to a mean wealth of about $175,000, the average or median white household of those over 70 (the fiftieth percentile) has $90,000 in wealth.

The enormous wealth inequality in America has little to do with race or ethnic issues. Even among whites, household wealth disparities are large. Whites at the top five percent have $655,000 in wealth, more than seven times that of the average white household. At the bottom, the lowest ten percent of white families has less than $1,000 in household wealth, less than one percent of the average household. Those white households at the 90th percentile have 60 times more wealth than white households at the 10th percentile.

Although unequal wealth is not at its core a racial or ethnic issue, this inequality reveals itself in especially stark ways when we make racial and

---

[6]For the purposes of this chart, households were ranked from bottom to top based on their household wealth. Separate rankings were performed within race and ethnic groups.

ethnic comparisons. There are a significant fraction of minority households that have no household wealth of which to speak. The median older black and Hispanic household has less than $20,000 in wealth. More than one-quarter of blacks and one-third of hispanics have no wealth at all—a figure that is even more dramatic given how broad our wealth concept is. Remember wealth includes all net equity in homes.

Especially Large Inequities in Financial Assets

Financial assets in $ (ages 70+)

Percentiles of financial assets	White	Black	Hispanic
10	0	0	0
20	157	0	0
30	1,500	0	0
50	10,500	0	0
70	45,000	1,000	750
90	172,500	11,000	14,600
95	300,000	32,300	45,000
Mean	*65,116*	*6,040*	*8,355*

Once again, more dramatic numbers appear when we consider only financial wealth. Neither the average older black nor the average older Hispanic household has any financial wealth at all—*not a dime*. Even the bottom third of older white families has less than $2,000 in liquid assets at their disposal, and one in five has less than $200.

Disparities Large Even in Preretirement Years

Percentiles of financial assets	Financial assets in $ (ages 51 – 61)		
	White	Black	Hispanic
10	0	0	0
20	800	0	0
30	3,000	0	0
50	17,300	400	150
70	53,000	5,000	3,000
90	174,500	33,250	30,000
95	300,000	58,000	56,000
Mean	*72,571*	*12,780*	*10,585*

The situation is a little different if we look at those in their preretirement years. More than four in ten middle-age black and Hispanic households have no liquid assets, and the typical such households have less than $500.

Income differences

Inheritances

Marital status

Health

Asset tests in means-tested social insurance programs

Replacement rates through social insurance and pensions

These then are the basic facts we must try to explain: modest wealth holdings by the typical household, large inequities in wealth, and very little evidence of any savings behavior by poorer households.

This chart lists some possible reasons for the low wealth accumulation among the poor. The most basic reason and a good place to start is that the poor simply have less income to devote to savings. Wealthier individuals may also have benefited by financial inheritances from their parents, implying that wealth inequalities may be transmitted across generations. For a number of reasons, households may save at different rates. Two reasons that turn out to be important are whether households include married couples, and how good the health of their members is. Finally, the existing structure of public policy may simply encourage poorer households not to save. In the remainder of the briefing, I go through these possibilities in sequence.

Income Explains Only Part of Wealth Disparities

Percentiles of household wealth	Wealth (relative to median)	Wealth/income ratio (relative to median)
10	0.01	0.03
20	0.14	0.26
30	0.42	0.62
50	1.00	1.00
70	1.89	1.18
90	4.56	1.59
95	7.24	1.81

(whites, ages 70+)

To what extent can income disparities account for the wealth inequalities we have documented?

This chart addresses this issue by first expressing household wealth inequality relative to the median household for older white families. To obtain the numbers in the second column, I simply divided household wealth at that percentile by the household wealth of the median or average household (the 50th percentile).

Household wealth of whites in the top five percent is seven times that of the median white household, whereas wealth of those at the bottom tenth is only one percent of the median. The adjacent column adjusts these ratios for income differences among households.[7] If income differences fully explained wealth differences (that is, if wealth were proportional to income), these ratios in the third column would all be 1. That clearly is not the case. After controlling for income differences, those in the top five percent now have 1.8 times the wealth of the median household.

Income does a pretty good job of explaining wealth disparities of those at the top, but income alone explains much less of the absence of wealth

_____
[7]The numbers in the third column are the wealth/income ratios at each percentile relative to the relative wealth/income ratio of the median household.

among those at the bottom. For example, among those at the 20th percentile, households save one-seventh of the median household. Even after adjusting for their income differences, these households at the bottom save only one-fourth of the average family. Clearly, the message is that income explains a significant part, but certainly not all of wealth disparities that exist, especially among the poor. The rest flows from the much lower savings rate for low income households compared with those with higher incomes. The remainder of this briefing explores some reasons why this may be so.

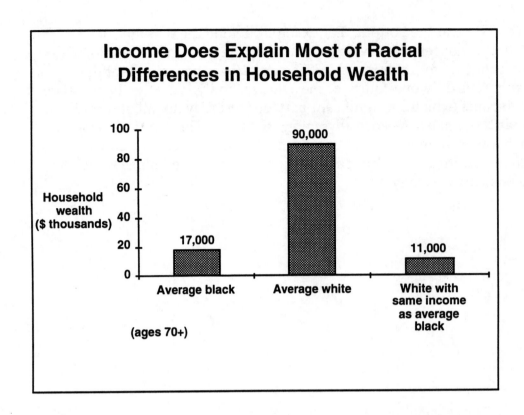

Income Does Explain Most of Racial Differences in Household Wealth

Household wealth ($ thousands)

Average black — 17,000
Average white — 90,000
White with same income as average black — 11,000

(ages 70+)

Before doing that, however, there is one piece of unfinished business regarding income. We know that there are very large racial and ethnic differences in wealth. This chart shows, however, that income explains most of the racial differences in wealth. It compares the median black to a white household with the same income. Although vastly less than the wealth of the average white, the household wealth of the median black is actually quite similar to a white household with the same income. Low savings behavior is not then a racial or ethnic issue. In spite of all the talk about distinct cultural histories that may explain why some ethnic or racial groups do not save, there is little evidence in favor of such an approach. The fundamental question instead is why low income people save so little no matter what their race and ethnic backgrounds.

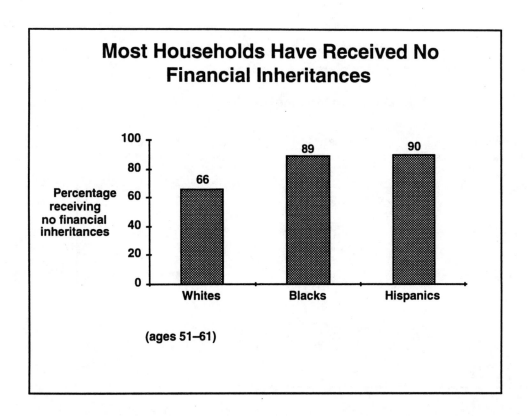

Most Households Have Received No Financial Inheritances

Percentage receiving no financial inheritances

(ages 51–61)

Before turning to savings behavior, there is an important question that must be addressed. Couldn't these wealth inequities simply be a consequence of wealth being transmitted across generations with the poor unable to give and the well-to-do insuring that their heirs remain at the top through financial inheritances? Although plausible, it turns out that this possibility is quantitatively unimportant. One reason is that the vast majority of these households have not received any financial inheritances. For example, two-thirds of all white households and 90 percent of all minority households had received no financial inheritances by their members' mid-fifties.

Inheritances Are Not Important for Wealth Inequities

Household wealth in $ (ages 51–61)

Percentiles of household wealth	Household wealth	Household wealth minus inheritance
10	923	923
20	16,352	10,969
30	39,563	33,919
50	97,506	89,739
70	193,152	179,143
90	504,278	469,378
95	843,598	780,641

My central point that financial inheritances have little to do with wealth inequalities in this country is dramatized most forcefully if we eliminate the influence of financial inheritances from the wealth distribution. This chart shows the inequities in wealth would be almost the same if we subtracted out that part of current wealth that flowed from past financial inheritances. More than 90 percent of current wealth inequalities have nothing to do with financial inheritances. If it is not financial inheritances, then all we have left is people saving at different rates from their income. Why would this be so?

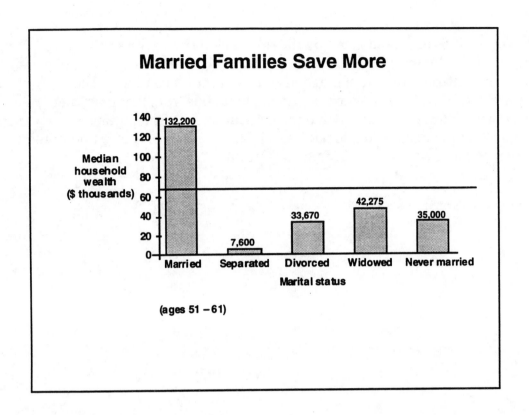

Married Families Save More

Median household wealth ($ thousands)

140 — 132,200

Married	Separated	Divorced	Widowed	Never married
132,200	7,600	33,670	42,275	35,000

Marital status

(ages 51 – 61)

One perhaps surprising reason is marriage. Poor families are more likely to divorce and less quick to remarry. Also, large fractions of black families in particular are headed by a single parent. What effect does marriage have on wealth accumulation?

The obvious direct impact is that the assets of two people are combined when married and are divided between two households when a divorce or separation takes place. This combination is important, but the above chart, which shows wealth by marital status, indicates that there is a lot more to it than that. If the blending of assets when individuals marry were all that was happening, then assets of married couples would be twice as large as that of other household types. In all cases, assets of people in nonmarried households are much less than half of those of couples in married households.

The one-half figure is indicated by the solid line drawn across this chart. For example, the wealth of a household headed by a separated person is about one-fifteenth of that of married couples in this age range. The implication is, and my research documents that it is true, that marriage strongly encourages savings behavior.[8] As an aside, this result also implies that the decline in marriage as a institution has played a role in the secular fall in the aggregate savings rate in this country.

—————

[8]For my details on the issue of marriage and savings, see Smith (1995b).

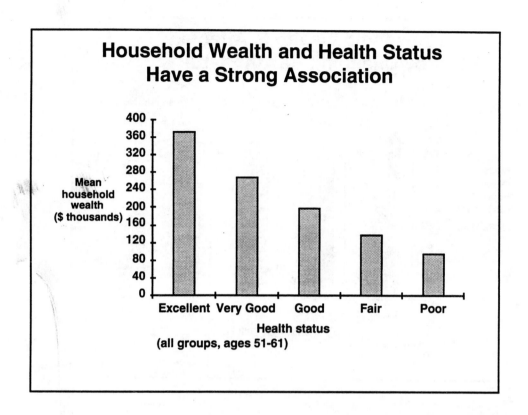

Household Wealth and Health Status Have a Strong Association

Mean household wealth ($ thousands)

Health status
(all groups, ages 51-61)

The next critical factor is health. Poor health reduces wealth for a number of reasons. First, those in poor health are less able to work at all and, if they do work, they do so for fewer hours. This work effect directly reduces income and savings. Households with a person in poor health also face higher medical expenses, further depleting their ability to save.

This chart demonstrates how strong the association between health status and wealth can be. Among those in stable health, those in excellent health have more than four times the wealth of those in poor health. Each step down in health leads to a significantly lower wealth.

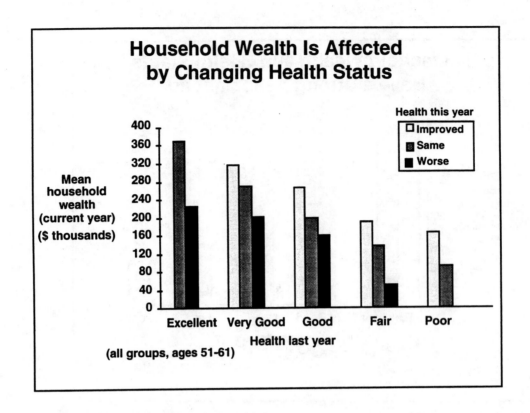

Household Wealth Is Affected by Changing Health Status

Mean household wealth (current year) ($ thousands)

Health this year
☐ Improved
▨ Same
■ Worse

Excellent   Very Good   Good   Fair   Poor

Health last year

(all groups, ages 51-61)

But it is not only current health that influences wealth. An improvement in health increases assets, whereas a health decline reduces wealth. For example, consider those who were in good health last year, the middle part of this graph. Compared with those whose health remained the same—that is, they were still in good health this year—those whose health improved had $80,000 more in wealth, but those whose health got worse had about $40,000 less in wealth.

The precise numbers vary, but the ranking remains the same no matter what health status prevailed in the prior years—improvements in health are associated with higher wealth levels, and deterioration in health is correlated with lower wealth.[9]

---

[9]An important question not addressed in this slide is the direction of causation between health and wealth. One can make good a priori arguments about each pathway of causation. For example, wealthier households may be able to purchase a more healthy lifestyle or more medical care, either one of which could lead to better health. Similarly, poor health can reduce income and wealth because of rising medical expenses, lower wages, or reduced labor supply. Smith and Kington (1995) demonstrate that the association between contemporaneous income and current health almost exclusively flows from health to income. The relative importance of the two-way mechanism for the long-run association is an open research question.

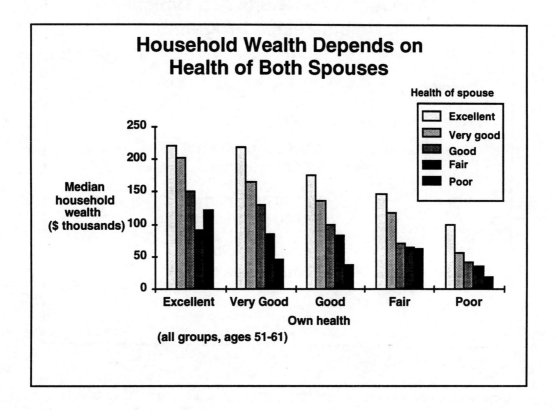

Household Wealth Depends on Health of Both Spouses

Median household wealth ($ thousands)

Health of spouse
- Excellent
- Very good
- Good
- Fair
- Poor

Own health

(all groups, ages 51-61)

Finally, my research demonstrates that the health of both spouses is equally important. For example, if we compare households with both spouses in excellent health to those in which both spouses are in poor health, assets vary by a factor of almost ten to one. Lower health of either spouse significantly reduces household wealth. The magnitude of these differences is truly impressive. Median wealth in households where both spouses are in poor health is about $25,000, compared with a median worth of over $200,000 when both spouses are in excellent health.[10]

---

[10]I have switched to the use of medians instead of means in this chart because the smaller sample sizes in some of the cells in this chart make the means volatile due to measurement error.

Stringent Asset Tests Are Typical in Means-Tested Programs

Program	Asset Limit
AFDC	$1,000
Food Stamp	$2,000 (nonelderly) $3,000 (elderly)
SSI	$2,000 (nonmarried) $3,000 (married)
Medicaid	(must be eligible for Food Stamps or SSI)

Unfortunately, public policy has also played a contributing role in providing incentives for the poor not to save. The two most important ways in which current policy discourages the poor not to save are asset tests contained in many of the safety net programs and high replacement rates in existing programs. Let me discuss each in turn.

Many of our safety net programs include asset tests that state that if current household assets exceed some specified amount, the household will fail to qualify for participation in the program.[11] This chart illustrates how stringent these asset limits can be in some typical programs.[12] Typically, some forms of wealth—usually housing and cars—are excluded from the test. Even with these exclusions, the actual asset cut-off point that will make a household ineligible is shockingly low.

For example, it is only $1,000 for AFDC. What incentive does a poor family with $800 in assets have to save an extra few hundred dollars over

---

[11]This argument has been advanced most cogently recently by Hubbard, Skinner, and Zeldes (1995).

[12]In this chart, AFDC represents Aid to Families with Dependent Children, while SSI is the Supplemental Security Income program.

the next few years to safeguard against some unforeseen emergency? Since it would render them ineligible for this important program, this otherwise prudent behavior would be quite foolish indeed.

One reason that the poor do not save is that we give them every reason not to. Note also the implicit incentive not to marry since the asset tests for married couples are never twice that of singles. Consider two people, each with assets of $1,800, considering whether to marry. Each individual is eligible for SSI benefits (they are below the $2,000 threshold), but as a couple they far exceed the $3,000 limit for married couples.

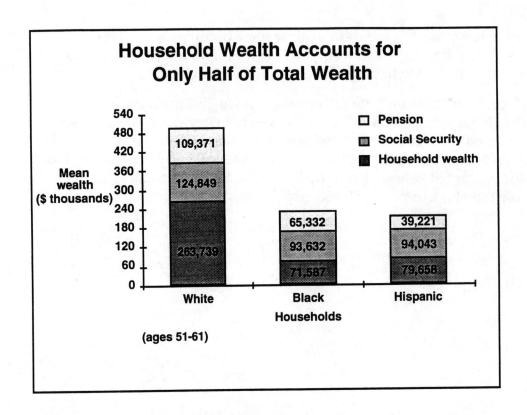

Household Wealth Accounts for Only Half of Total Wealth

Mean wealth ($ thousands)

	Pension	Social Security	Household wealth
White	109,371	124,849	263,739
Black	65,332	93,632	71,587
Hispanic	39,221	94,043	79,658

Households

(ages 51-61)

As mentioned earlier, household wealth ignores critical components of wealth that can loom large, especially for these households in their preretirement and postretirement years. I will illustrate the point with the sample of those households in their fifties. Virtually, all of these households anticipate a flow of Social Security benefits when they retire. More than half of them are also counting on the income from their pensions. When discounted to the present, these expected income flows translate into considerable amounts of wealth.

This chart demonstrates how large the wealth from these sources actually is. For each of our groups, mean levels of household, Social Security, and pension wealth are listed. This chart makes a number of fundamental points. First, the widely used conventional household wealth concept hides half of the iceberg. Combined, Social Security and pension wealth are as important as household wealth for these families. Total white household wealth is almost half a million dollars instead of the roughly quarter of a million that we saw earlier. Second, this distortion caused by the conventional wealth concept is much larger among minority families. Among blacks and Hispanics, conventional household wealth is less than a third of their total wealth. For minority households, Social Security wealth is especially critical and represents the largest part of their wealth, a subject to which I will soon return.

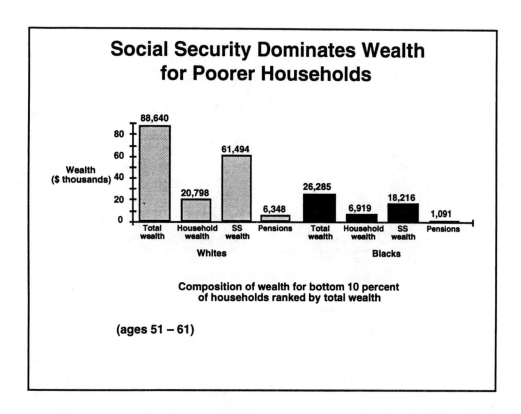

Social Security Dominates Wealth for Poorer Households

Wealth ($ thousands)

Whites: Total wealth 88,640; Household wealth 20,798; SS wealth 61,494; Pensions 6,348

Blacks: Total wealth 26,285; Household wealth 6,919; SS wealth 18,216; Pensions 1,091

Composition of wealth for bottom 10 percent of households ranked by total wealth

(ages 51 – 61)

The fundamental importance of social security for low income households is dramatized more starkly in this chart, which lists components of wealth for households who rank at the bottom ten percent in total wealth. For both white and black households in this situation, Social Security is the dominant form of wealth.[13] In a nutshell, it is basically the only wealth they have. Seventy percent of the total wealth of these households rests in their future Social Security checks. As you can see, very few of these households have any pensions either in their past or future.

---

[13]In contrast to the chart on page 7, these households at the bottom do have positive amounts of household wealth. The reason for this difference is that households in the chart on this page are ranked according to their total wealth.

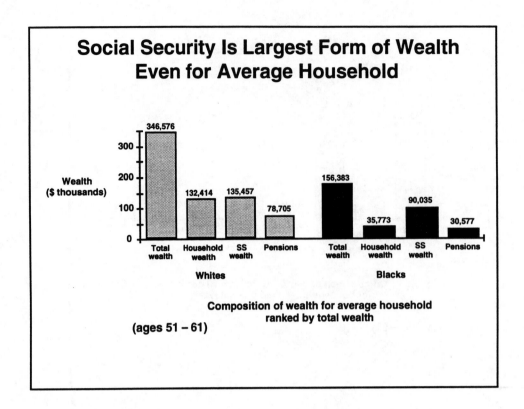

**Social Security Is Largest Form of Wealth
Even for Average Household**

Wealth
($ thousands)

	Whites				Blacks		
Total wealth	Household wealth	SS wealth	Pensions	Total wealth	Household wealth	SS wealth	Pensions
346,576	132,414	135,457	78,705	156,383	35,773	90,035	30,577

Composition of wealth for average household
ranked by total wealth

(ages 51 – 61)

While less extreme, Social Security still wins first place in the wealth portfolio even for the median household. The median white household headed by middle-age people has more Social Security wealth than either household wealth (including their home) or pensions. It is not even a close call for the typical black household, which has more wealth in Social Security than household and pension wealth combined.

26

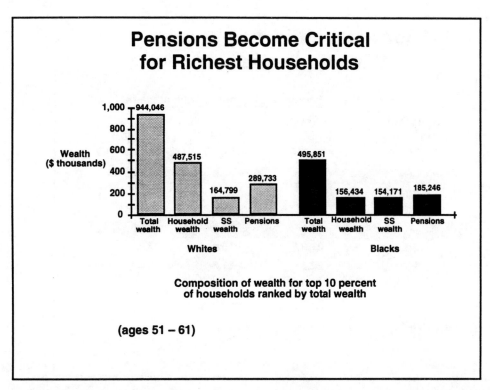

**Pensions Become Critical
for Richest Households**

Composition of wealth for top 10 percent
of households ranked by total wealth

(ages 51 – 61)

Life on the other side of the tracks is different. This chart illustrates wealth holdings for households with the top ten percent of total wealth. Not only is total wealth considerably higher, the composition has shifted dramatically toward household wealth and pensions. Pension wealth is now large both absolutely and as a fraction of the total, accounting for about almost a third of total wealth. These top 10 percent households have about three times as much pension wealth alone as the total wealth of those households at the bottom.

It is important to note that Social Security wealth of these households is not that different from the median household. This is a remarkable result given how far apart these people are in the income distribution. In a way, it summarizes the political and substantive power of Social Security. For those receiving or about to receive Social Security, in wealth terms, they are receiving a lot of money that often dwarfs any other wealth they might ever hope to have. The substantive success is that Social Security is a highly redistributive system.[14]

_____

[14]The dimension in which Social Security is not progressive—the association of income and longevity—is not taken into account in these numbers.

Poor Have Little Incentive to
Save for Retirement

Household Income Percentile	Percentage of household income replaced		
	Pension	Social Security	Pension + Social Security
5	10.8	81.6	92.4
10	13.4	59.1	72.5
20	16.7	42.1	58.8
50	21.3	24.1	45.3
80	21.8	15.4	37.3
90	22.3	11.3	33.5
95	19.6	9.4	29.0

(ages 51–61)

This chart, which contains income replacement rates from pensions and Social Security, illustrates the downside of our current Social Security system. These replacement rates are the fraction of household income that will be replaced by pensions and Social Security at the time the household retires. To illustrate with an example, let's say the median household in this age group currently earns $38,000, which is about what it does. This household will receive about $17,000 in Social Security and pensions when it retires, 45 percent of its current income. The big news, however, is the sharply declining replacement rates with income and the very high rates for low income households. Over 90 percent of the current income of those at the bottom five percent will be replaced, but only 29 percent of the incomes of those at the top will be. Social Security is clearly responsible for this sharp decline, replacing over 80 percent of income of those at the bottom.

This chart actually understates the extent of replacement since I have also not taken into account any of the income-conditioned safety net programs available to these households when they are older, such as SSI, food stamps, Medicare, and Medicaid. It is not an exaggeration to say that these households may be better off when they retire than they are now. In that sense, current public policy has over-annuitized our set of transfer programs since many of these households would prefer more money now at the expense of a little less in the future. Most important, the incentives these households have to save for their own retirement is almost nil.

This result turns some of our earlier data somewhat on their head. One reason that low income households have accumulated little private wealth of their own is that they have little incentive to do so.

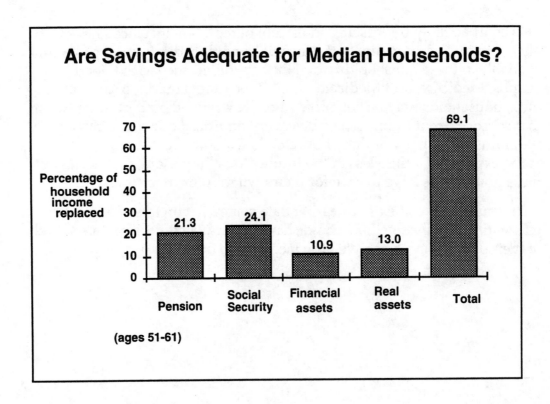

Are Savings Adequate for Median Households?

Percentage of household income replaced

Pension 21.3
Social Security 24.1
Financial assets 10.9
Real assets 13.0
Total 69.1

(ages 51-61)

The next question I address is whether savings are adequate for those who are now in their preretirement years. This chart repeats the pension and Social Security replacement rates for the median household. The adjacent bars represent the percentage of income from their financial savings and from their real assets that they will be able to replace when they retire.

The final bar indicates that from all these sources the average household with members in their fifties will be able to replace 69 percent of its income, with only a third of this flowing from private household savings. This figure actually understates replacement because I have not taken into account that a large fraction of Social Security income is not taxed. Will this be enough?

There is no unambiguous answer to this question, but my own assessment is, that from all these sources, the typical household has provided sufficiently for its retirement years. The money consumption needs of older households fall when they retire in part because they no longer have to pay work-related expenses, all will have subsidized health care through Medicare, and they can substitute their time for money and enjoy an expanding array of price discounts related to age.

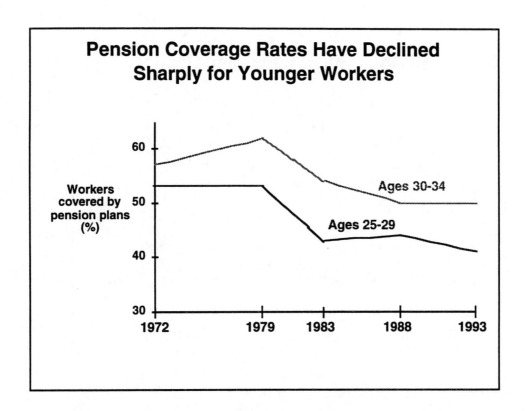

Pension Coverage Rates Have Declined Sharply for Younger Workers

Workers covered by pension plans (%)

Ages 30-34

Ages 25-29

60

50

40

30

1972   1979   1983   1988   1993

Although the verdict is cautiously positive for those households headed by middle-age people, alarm bells should ring when our attention shifts to households of people born in the peak of the baby boom. For these households, pension prevalence rates have already started to decline, reversing almost a century-old trend. Throughout this century, each generation of workers has enjoyed greater access to private pensions that provided some cushion for their retirement years. In the last 20 years, that trend reversed for those workers less than 35 years old. Pension prevalence rates for those workers under 30 fell by almost ten percentage points since the early 1970s. Add on that our current Social Security promises are impossible to keep in the future. Not only do we know it, younger generations know it.

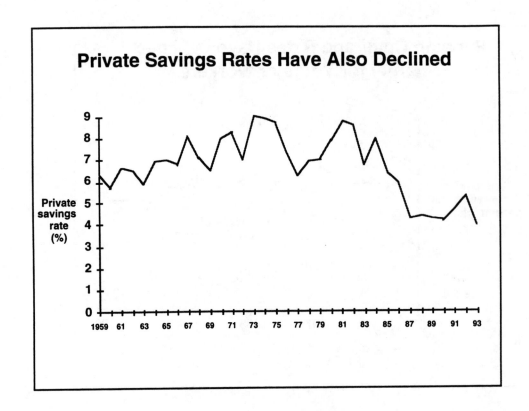

Private Savings Rates Have Also Declined

Two legs of the retirement tier are thus guaranteed to fall. What about the third leg—private savings? Here the early evidence is also not promising. Savings rates for all age groups have fallen sharply during the last decade, providing the well documented decline in the national savings rate. These younger generations may actually be saving at lower rates than their predecessors.

```
┌─────────────────────────────────────────────────┐
│                                                   │
│              Public Policy Options                │
│                                                   │
│                                                   │
│     • Make realistic promises about future public│
│       support                                     │
│                                                   │
│     • Initiate bold moves to encourage private savings│
│        – Consumption tax                          │
│                                                   │
│        – Mandatory Provident-type fund            │
│                                                   │
│     • Change asset limits in means-tested programs│
│                                                   │
│                                                   │
└─────────────────────────────────────────────────┘
```

What can be done? At one level, the overwhelming dimensions of the problems make the outline of the solution clear, although we all know how difficult politically the solutions will be to implement.

For openers,[15] we will have to start making realistic promises about our public support system and to focus public efforts only on ensuring a decent standard of living for the elderly poor. It has been estimated that our current Social Security and Medicare promises alone would imply an average tax rate of 80 percent in the next century.

First, our long-run policy goal should be to start turning our public support system into a sustainable system with the twin but limited goals of reducing old age poverty and coinsuring against some multiple risks, including poor health. This policy goal implies that Social Security should not be viewed as the prime source of retirement income replacement across all income levels. Rather, it should provide a minimum decent standard of living in old age. We can accomplish this goal through different ways, a means-tested benefit or a universal flat benefit, but

---

[15]These recommendations were heavily influenced by an excellent World Bank report (1994) on the aging crisis.

accomplish it we must. Second, realism must also enter our legitimate provision of health insurance for the elderly population. Even more so than Social Security, our current health care promises are not sustainable.

Once again, for the elderly there are legitimate areas of disagreement about how to accomplish this aim. But the guiding principle should be to provide insurance for the real health care risks and not full subsidies for everyone.

With the inevitable decline in our dependence on a pay-as-you-go Social Security system, we must strengthen the private support for old age through additional private savings. Given the daunting dimensions of our future problems, our guiding principle here must be to be bold—no tinkering at the margin will do. Again, there are legitimate disagreements about the direction to follow, but the need for boldness pushes us toward a consumption tax to voluntarily encourage savings or a mandatory Provident-type fund that deducts a certain percentage of income for future retirement.

The policy debate about the consumption tax often confuses two separate issues—taxing wealth, and taxing the creation of wealth. By exempting savings and investments from taxation, the fundamental rationale for a consumption tax is that it does not tax the creation of wealth, thereby encouraging economic growth. Finally, we must review all our means-tested programs with an eye toward relaxing or eliminating assets tests that encourage the poor not to save.

Policy Issues

- **Are households saving enough for their retirement years?**

- **Does our current Social Security system reduce private savings?**

- **Do our existing safety net programs encourage the poor not to save?**

- **How important are inheritances in solidifying inequalities across generations?**

What then are our answers to the policy questions raised at the beginning of this briefing? Are households saving enough for their retirement years? An optimistic "yes" for the generation currently in their preretirement years, but loud alarm bells are ringing for the future. Does our current Social Security system reduce private savings? The magnitude of the trade-off is uncertain, but there is little question that our pay-as-you-go system eliminates some private savings. The poor especially are encouraged not to save both because of extremely stringent asset tests alongside high replacement rates from Social Security. Finally, inheritances have little to do with the extreme wealth inequalities in this country. Rather they stem from different savings behavior. Saving must be encouraged for all segments of the population.

BIBLIOGRAPHY

Hubbard, Glenn, Jon Skinner, and Steven Zeldes. 1995. "Precautionary Savings and Social Insurance," *Journal of Political Economy*, Vol. 103, No. 2, pp. 361-399.

Hurd, Michael, Willard Rodgers, Beth Soldo, and Robert Wallace. 1994. "Asset and Health Dynamics Among the Oldest Old: An Overview of the Survey," unpublished paper.

Juster, F. Thomas, and James P. Smith. 1995. *Improving the Quality of Economic Data: Lessons from the HRS*, RAND DRU-988-NIA, Labor and Population Program Working Paper 95-05.

Juster, F. Thomas, and Richard Suzman. 1995. "The Health and Retirement Survey: An Overview," *Journal of Human Resources*, forthcoming.

Smith, James P. 1995a. "Racial Differences in Wealth," *Journal of Human Resources*, forthcoming.

Smith, James P. 1995b. *Marriage, Assets, and Savings*, RAND DRU-1055-NIA, Labor and Population Program Working Paper 95-08.

Smith, James P. 1995c. *Wealth Inequality Among Older Americans*, RAND DRU-989-NIA, Labor and Population Program Working Paper 95-06.

Smith, James P., and Raynard Kington. 1995. *Race, Socioeconomic Status, and Health in Late Life*, RAND DRU-1063-NIA/NICHD, Labor and Population Program Working Paper 95-10.

Wolff, Edward N. 1994. "Trends in Household Wealth in the United States, 1962-83 and 1983-89," *Review of Income and Wealth*, Vol. 400, pp. 143-174.

World Bank. 1994. "Averting the Old Age Crisis," *World Bank Policy Research Report*, Oxford University Press.

DB-145-RC

ISBN 0-8330-2289-X